GETTING AROUND IN MY TOWN

TAKING A RIDESHARE

By Owen Hamlin

Consultant: Beth Gambro
Reading Specialist, Yorkville, Illinois

BEARPORT PUBLISHING

Minneapolis, Minnesota

Teaching Tips

Before Reading

- Look at the cover of the book. Discuss the picture and the title.
- Ask readers to brainstorm a list of what they already know about taking a rideshare. What can they expect to see in the book?
- Go on a picture walk, looking through the pictures to discuss vocabulary and make predictions about the text.

During Reading

- Read for purpose. Encourage readers to think about the kinds of ways they can get around in their town.
- Ask readers to look for the details of the book. What are the steps to taking a rideshare?
- If readers encounter an unknown word, ask them to look at the sounds in the word. Then, ask them to look at the rest of the page. Are there any clues to help them understand?

After Reading

- Encourage readers to pick a buddy and reread the book together.
- Ask readers to name two things they might do while taking a rideshare. Find the pages that tell about these things.
- Ask readers to write or draw something they learned about taking a rideshare.

Credits
Cover and title page, © bruev/iStock and © whitebalance.oatt/iStock; 3, © ZakS Photography/Adobe Stock; 5, © Michael Vi/iStock; 7, © adamkaz/iStock; 8–9, © SolStock/iStock; 11, © Andrzej Tokarski/Adobe Stock, © venusangel/Adobe Stock, © Lemonsoup14/Adobe Stock, © Pixel-Shot/Adobe Stock, © artisteer/iStock, and © Michael Burrell/iStock; 12–13, © Mat Hayward/Adobe Stock; 15, © algre/Adobe Stock, © whitebalance.oatt/iStock, and © Anchiy/iStock; 16–17, © Tada Images/Adobe Stock; 19, © Volonoff/Shutterstock, © agrobacter/iStock, and © TriggerPhoto/iStock; 21, © Sean2008/iStock and © AHMET YARALI/iStock; 22, © Alekss/Adobe Stock, © adamkaz/iStock, and © jetcityimage/Adobe Stock; 23TL, © Kaspars Grinvalds/Adobe Stock; 23TR, © nanskyblack/Adobe Stock; 23BL, © Kaspars Grinvalds/Adobe Stock; 23BR, © Alex/Adobe Stock.

See BearportPublishing.com for our statement on Generative AI Usage.

Library of Congress Cataloging-in-Publication Data

Names: Hamlin, Owen, 2000- author.
Title: Taking a rideshare / by Owen Hamlin.
Description: Minneapolis, Minnesota : Bearport Publishing Company, [2025] |
Series: Getting around in my town | Includes bibliographical references
and index.
Identifiers: LCCN 2024024994 (print) | LCCN 2024024995 (ebook) | ISBN
9798892326292 (library binding) | ISBN 9798892327091 (paperback) | ISBN
9798892326698 (ebook)
Subjects: LCSH: Ridesharing--Juvenile literature. |
Transportation--Juvenile literature. | CYAC: Ridesharing. |
transportation.
Classification: LCC HE5620.R53 H35 2025 (print) | LCC HE5620.R53 (ebook)
| DDC 388.3/21--dc23/eng/20240701
LC record available at https://lccn.loc.gov/2024024994
LC ebook record available at https://lccn.loc.gov/2024024995

For more information, write to Bearport Publishing, 5357 Penn Avenue South, Minneapolis, MN 55419.

Contents

Beep, Beep!

Today, we are going to the beach.

How will we get there?

We need someone to drive us.

Let's take a rideshare!

Say rideshare like RIDE-shair

Rideshares **connect** drivers with people who need rides.

A driver picks us up in their car.

They take us where we need to go.

We open a rideshare **app**.

This is how we find a car.

We type in where we want to go.

And we enter where we are.

There are many drivers that can take us.

But we need one with a big car.

We have lots of things for the beach!

The app shows us how much the ride will cost.

We tap a button to **order** the car.

The driver is on their way.

Economy
Affordable, everyday rides
UberX
$73.45
12:08pm
Comfort
$93.88
12:10pm
Confirm UberX
1-4

We look at the app as we wait.

It tells us the car is red.

Our driver is named Owen.

Now, we know what to look for.

Driver: Owen

Buzz!

The app lets us know our driver is here.

The car has a sticker in the window.

This shows it is a rideshare.

Uber
710443
lyft

We put our things in the **trunk**.

Then, we set off.

The driver uses a map on their phone.

It tells them where to go.

AUDIO CTRL
TUNE·FILE
SEEK
TRACK
TA
AF
AST
1
2
3
4
5
6
PTY
TEXT
AM
FM
DISC
A/C

I can see the beach.

We made it!

Thank you, driver.

I love taking a rideshare.

Parts of a Rideshare

A rideshare gets us around our town. Let's look at its parts.

Glossary

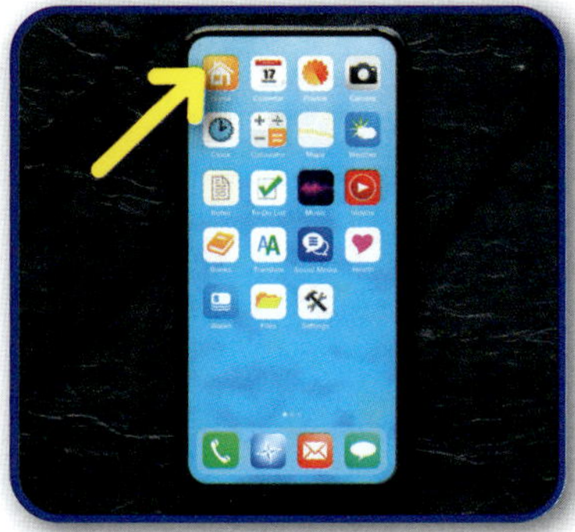

app something on a phone that lets people do a task

connect to join together

order to ask for something

trunk a space at the back of a car where you can put things

Index

Read More

Duling, Kaitlyn. *Cars (Blastoff! Readers: How It Works).* Minneapolis: Bellwether Media, Inc., 2022.

Kelly, Miranda. *Cars Go! (My First Transportation Books).* New York: Crabtree Publishing Company, 2023.

Learn More Online

1. Go to **FactSurfer.com** or scan the QR code below.
2. Enter "**Taking a Rideshare**" into the search box.
3. Click on the cover of this book to see a list of websites.

About the Author

Owen has never taken a rideshare before. He is glad he knows how to now!